Comparing

Minibeast
Food

Charlotte Guillai

Raintree

www.raintreepublishers.co.uk
Visit our website to find out
more information about
Raintree books.

To order:
☎ Phone 0845 6044371
▤ Fax +44 (0) 1865 312263
✉ Email myorders@raintreepublishers.co.uk

Customers from outside the UK please telephone +44 1865 312262

Raintree is an imprint of Capstone Global Library Limited, a company
incorporated in England and Wales having its registered office at 7 Pilgrim
Street, London, EC4V 6LB – Registered company number: 6695582

Text © Capstone Global Library Limited 2010
First published in hardback in 2010
Paperback edition first published in 2011
The moral rights of the proprietor have been asserted.

Edited by Nancy Dickmann and Catherine Veitch
Designed by Joanna Hinton-Malivoire
Picture research by Elizabeth Alexander
Production by Duncan Gilbert and Victoria Fitzgerald
Originated by Heinemann Library
Printed and bound in China by South China Printing
Company Ltd

ISBN 978 0 431 19494 3 (hardback)
14 13 12 11 10
10 9 8 7 6 5 4 3 2 1

ISBN 978 0 431 19501 8 (paperback)
15 14 13 12 11
10 9 8 7 6 5 4 3 2 1

British Library Cataloguing in Publication Data
Guillain, Charlotte.
Comparing minibeasts.
Food.
592.1'53-dc22

Acknowledgements
We would would like to thank the following for permission to reproduce
photographs: Alamy pp. **4** (© Roger Eritja), **15** (© blickwinkel), **17**
(© blickwinkel), **16** (© B. Mete Uz); Ardea.com pp. **13** (© John Daniels),
18 (© Pascal Goetgheluck); Corbis pp. **9** (© Steffen Schmidt/epa), **23
bottom** (© Steffen Schmidt/epa); FLPA p. **19** (© Heidi & Hans-Juergen
Koch); Getty Images p. **8** (George Grall/National Geographic); iStockphoto
pp. **5** (© andrey Pavlov), **6** (© Michal Boubin), **11** (© Robert Kobsa), **22
top right**; NHPA p. **20** (A.N.T. Photo Library); Photolibrary pp. **7** (Patti
Murray/Animals Animals); RSPCA p. **19** (Tim Martin); Shutterstock pp. **10**
(© Cathleen Clapper), **12** (© Kletr), **14** (© Johan Swanepoel), **22 top left**
(© alle), **22 bottom left** (© alle), **22 bottom right** (© Eric Isselée), **23
top** (© Yellowj).

Cover photograph of a caterpillar (European Swallowtail) feeding on carrot
leaves reproduced with permission of Ardea (© Steve Hopkin). Back cover
photograph of beetles rolling a ball of dung in South Africa reproduced with
permission of Shutterstock (© Johan Swanepoel).

The publishers would like to thank Nancy Harris and Kate Wilson for their
assistance in the preparation of this book.

Every effort has been made to contact copyright holders of material
reproduced in this book. Any omissions will be rectified in subsequent
printings if notice is given to the publishers.

Contents

Meet the minibeasts

There are many different types of minibeasts.

Minibeasts eat many
different foods.

Plants

Most minibeasts get their food from plants.

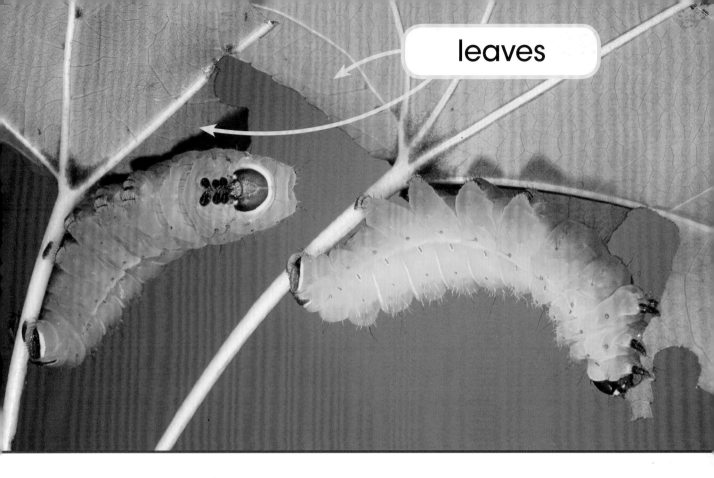

leaves

Most caterpillars eat leaves.

dead wood

Woodlice eat dead wood.

pollen

Bees eat pollen from flowers.

seed

Milkweed bugs eat seeds.

fruit

Some wasps eat fruit.

Blood and poo

Some mosquitoes suck blood from animals. Then they fly away.

Ticks suck blood from animals.
Then they drop off.

poo

Dung beetles eat poo.

poo

Many flies eat poo, too.

Eating other animals

grasshopper

Some wasps eat other insects.

blackfly

Ladybirds eat blackflies.

A praying mantis might eat another
praying mantis.

Some spiders eat other spiders.

Some minibeasts eat larger animals.

Some big centipedes eat mice.

How big?

beetle

earwig

caterpillar

spider

Look at how big some of the minibeasts in this book can be.

Picture glossary

insect very small creature with six legs

pollen golden powder inside flowers

Index

Notes to parents and teachers

Before reading

Make a list of minibeasts with the children. Try to include insects, arachnids (e.g. spiders), crustaceans (e.g. woodlice), myriapods (e.g. centipedes and millipedes), earthworms, slugs, and snails. Do they know what each minibeast eats? Ask them to make suggestions if they do not know and then read the book to see if they guessed correctly.

After reading

- Did the children find out what all the minibeasts on their list eat? If they are still not sure about any of them, use reference books or the Internet together to find the answers.
- If you have a garden in the school grounds, look at the plants between spring and late summer and see if any minibeasts are eating them. Are there any bees or butterflies visiting the flowers? Look for pollen on bees' legs and bodies. You can also look for signs that a minibeast has been feeding on a particular plant.
- Start a class wormery to observe what compost worms eat. Discuss how these worms help us to recycle waste and help the environment.